LIVING WITH NO REGRETS

Happy, Healthy Relationships in Love, Sex and Marriage

B. Charles Hostetter
with
James Fairfield

Choice Books
Harrisonburg, Virginia

LIVING WITH NO REGRETS
Happy, Healthy Relationships
in Love, Sex and Marriage

Revised edition

Published by Choice Books,
1251 Virginia Avenue
Harrisonburg, VA 22801

Choice Books are distributed exclusively
by Mennonite Board of Missions.

Originally published as
KEEP YOURSELF PURE
1957 by Moody Press

Cover photo Robert Cushman Hayes
Cover design Cheryl Lyon

Printed in United States of America

Contents

Preface

The Bible has some strong words about sexual indulgence. It has always been one of the most unmanageable problems for humanity. Few escape the urge to take sex when and where it can be found. As an instinctual drive, it is one of our strongest.

The power of sex to distort relationships shows up in story and legend throughout human history. No tribe, people, nation, or generation has gone unscarred by its demands. Every century has heard the appeal for sexual freedom in one way or another, and suffered the consequences. No wonder the Bible has so much to say about this universal condition.

During the summer of 1953 I spoke on the theme *Keep Yourself Pure*, on the international radio broadcasts of The Mennonite Hour. My purpose was to encourage listeners to a renewed respect for sexual integrity. The material in the radio broadcast became the book in its earliest editions. It has been reprinted widely throughout the English speaking world.

Now the revised version. I pray it will be of help to you in your life. The problem hasn't gone away, only changed its fashions. We will always struggle to channel our sexual energies. But it is in the struggle for integrity that we find the strength of God to live in his freedom and grace.

— B. Charles Hostetter

Thinking right about sex

1

It was a shock to hear the man was dead; the officials called it suicide. He was in his early thirties and a practicing physician. He had been very successful and had everything to live for, but he took his own life.

I remember clearly my last conversation with him, about five or six years earlier. He had vigorously defended the viewpoint that sexual intercourse for unmarried people was not wrong. He insisted that God had made us that way, and sex was a normal biological appetite like hunger or any other physical need. He contended that if both parties agreed and were careful enough to avoid pregnancy, sexual intercourse was no worse than kissing or any other social activity between the sexes.

He laughed at my defense of sexual integrity and scoffed at the Bible's view of sexual promiscuity as a hurtful sin. He refused to believe that sexual activity outside marriage creates enormous problems for those who engage in it.

I suggested to him that God knew the history of human temptation much better than he did, and that, unless he changed his thinking, he was setting himself against God. Again he laughed; to him the idea of God was a superstition and hopelessly out of date. For him, science and modern philosophy had established that morality is relative rather than absolute.

I suppose we talked an hour that day. Nothing I could say would convince him that sexual activity outside of marriage carried with it profound social and spiritual problems. To him I was simply behind the times, and hopelessly old fashioned in my belief in God .

Now he was dead. I wondered if he had ever questioned his unbelief—I hope so. Something had obviously shaken the man to the depth of his being.

Why is it that sexual integrity is considered old-fashioned? Today young people barely in their teens seem to get into sex as easily as actors in a soap opera. At least that's the conclusion we must come to in considering the number of teenage pregnancies in our "liberated" society.

If we are to believe the statisticians, few girls and fewer boys enter marriage as virgins. The exceptions are oddities, subjects for psychological analysis or off-color jokes.

A young friend of mine took a summer job in a large Detroit industry. He wanted to try out his Christian ideals and express his faith in a factory setting. If you've ever been there you know it's not the easiest environment for an idealistic youth. As he got to know his fellow workers, he sensed their disdain. And they sensed his difference.

Now it's a fact of life that most humans don't much like it when others are too different. We try to bring people down to our own level, and that's the way his fellow workers treated my young friend. They attempted to get a reaction from him with sexually explicit stories. He was urged to "break down and have a drink" with them after work—or *at* work. He was offered drugs. Some of the women openly attempted to seduce him.

One day as his workmates questioned him, he insisted he had kept his sexual integrity all his teenage years and now that he was twenty-one, he had no regrets. In fact, he intended to stay that way by the grace of God. Furthermore, he thought it was a good idea for anyone to live "purely," as he put it.

He was ridiculed, of course. But two or three of his co-workers were sufficiently impressed to comment on his tough-minded stand. One young man told him he had never met anyone with such a clear sense of values.

What does this say for our world? Not much. It suggests that the moral standards we have adopted are now about as low as at any time in history, and there have been some very low spots in the past. We look back at the decadence of the late Roman Empire and think that, because we are living in the nuclear age, we are morally superior.

Yet at no time in history have men and women engaged more freely in sexual activity. Part of the reason has to do with widespread availability of contraceptive methods, and abortion. We have even convinced ourselves that abortion has nothing to do with the taking of human life. We think we are morally "pure" even though what we are now doing has always and everywhere been considered morally wrong and abhorrent throughout enlightened human history.

What if we *are* wrong, and the Bible with its point of view is right? What if decency, restraint, clean mindedness and moral purity are really irreplaceable aspects of that characteristic we admire as integrity?

That we are not as morally mature as we think we are might help explain why we have so many broken marriages. Looking at it this way, we can't rely on the argument that people are psychologically healthier if they are able to move in and out of sexual relationships freely. That argument is of the same kind as the one supporting abortion and open marriages; it doesn't hold water. It never did or will.

Too many lonely mothers are looking after children on their own. Too many women who have had abortions are psychologically scarred. Too many children of broken marriages are themselves broken in spirit. Ask *them* if they are enjoying the fruits of our new found "freedoms."

No, the freedoms we are "enjoying" aren't nearly as freeing as we have been led to believe. Freedom without responsibility has never been freedom. Disobeying God's law can never be good for us, nor can we escape the consequences.

Yesterday's perspective

I am not a young man any more. Perhaps that will disqualify me in the eyes of some readers who do not believe that anyone much older than they are has anything relevant to say, particularly about sex. But such an assumption would be a serious mistake. Age may bring a decline in sexual drive, but age more than makes up for glandular frenzy with a measure of experienced capability. And I will never be so old—Lord willing—that I will not remember what it was like to be young.

What age can add, sometimes, is perspective. Age helps one see the end of the road that others have taken. Our modern way of doing things is not necessarily the *right* way. People talk of the "wisdom of the ages" because it has a long term perspective, and can see beyond the present.

For the moment, let the Bible speak its wisdom to us: we are led astray by the influences of the world around us. Other people try to force us into their mold. We may call it peer pressure; the Bible says we allow ourselves to be conformed to the "pattern of this world" (Romans 12:2 NIV). It's as if we haven't the spiritual stamina to be who God has designed us to be. Instead we succumb to what the world around us wants, we live according to its pattern and its pressures. Like the young man in the factory in Detroit, the "world" imposes a demand through everyone around us and it takes a life of faith to live otherwise.

We're also led astray by what the Bible calls our "flesh" or "heart" or "sinful nature." This isn't just a Christian or New Testament idea but reaches back into the early history of faith. The Lord God of Creation spoke of human nature through the prophet Jeremiah: "The heart is deceitful above all things and desperately corrupt" (Jeremiah 17:9 RSV). Isaiah, another prophet, is more outspoken. Even when we think that we are as good as we need to be, he says we are fooling ourselves and "all our righteous acts are like filthy rags" (Is. 64:6 NIV).

Harsh words for modern ears. We don't like to think of ourselves in those terms — we who believe we are good and in control of our lives and destinies. But are we? Suppose for the moment that the evil we see in the headlines day after day is simply the evidence of the corrupt hearts of mankind being caught in the act. The rest of us haven't been caught, yet. That is what I call a wisdom perspective, because it's a lot closer to the truth than any other. The New Testament repeats an Old Testament view in Romans 3:10-12:

"There is no one righteous, not even one...
All have turned away
and together become worthless.
There is no one who does good,
not even one" (NIV).

Another difficulty for modern ears—suppose there really is a "devil," a Satan, an evil force that pits itself against all that is of God? The Bible again insists upon something here that we don't accept easily in our highly sophisticated world.

But maybe that's the problem. The "world" convinces us that there is no such force because it's to the "world's" advantage for us to be deceived. That way we go along without being aware of the real nature of things, and we're unable to make the responses to set ourselves free. Why should we try to get free when we already believe we *are* "free"?

The Bible is very clear about this organized evil. We may think the only problems we have are with one or two people who seem bent on making life difficult for us, but the Bible goes further. Our struggle is not simply with flesh and blood (including our own),"...it is against organizations and powers that are spiritual. We are up against the unseen power that controls this dark world, and spiritual agents from the very headquarters of evil" (Ephesians 6:12, Phillips).

It's as if evil generates evil; anything obscene, underhanded, filthy minded, despicable, dishonest or malicious works overtime to reinforce every tendency we might have for wrongdoing. Let's call it what the Bible calls it—*sin*. Sin, of whatever kind and quantity, multiplies itself.

In a three way bind

The wisdom of the centuries understands our human condition. The old Book of Common Prayer called for deliverance from the world, the flesh, and the devil; from pressure to conform, from our own weaknesses, and from the relentless power of accumulated evil-calling-to-evil.

We are in a fearsome bind. We may want to live a better life (most people do unless they are so far gone in evil they no longer care) yet we don't seem to have the strength to do any better. In fact, we don't even know what to do in order to do right. When we were younger we may have had a vision of staying "good," of remaining pure, but now the reasons for doing so have faded from our minds, and we are swept along on the current of "the world, the flesh and the devil."

Let's be sure about our situation, whatever else it may be it is *not* freedom. It is not integrity. It is not morally justified. On the contrary, the situation in which a great many people find themselves right now is not freedom but bondage. Not integrity but its lack. Not morally stable but immorally insecure.

It's a helpless state to be in. But it needn't be the way to live the rest of our lives.

The world, the flesh, and the devil may assure you that sexual liberty is right—good because it feels good—but that is because the world, the flesh, and the devil conspire to operate on the basis of selfishness. This unholy trinity teaches you to ignore the effects of your actions on other persons. It urges you to enjoy yourself, and if someone else can happen to enjoy himself/herself at the same time, that's all you can hope to achieve.

In this case, sex becomes little more than mutual masturbation. But again listen to the Biblical wisdom: sex is for marriage alone. It belongs only within the lifelong commitment to give of yourself to your spouse. The implication is that sex is only a part of a much larger reality called commitment, and sex under any other circumstance is self indulgence.

Closer to the truth

I'm sorry if that sounds outrageous to you, but it is much closer to the truth than the monumental lies we have been handed from the media. What those lies can do to you is the subject of this book. But I won't leave you without hope; it is also part of the wisdom of the ages that the grace of God is sufficient to bring you full freedom.

You *can* stay sexually pure. What's more, the benefits of purity can enhance so greatly that you should read the rest of this book for that reason alone.

Remember, freedom is what it's about. The freedom Jesus insisted was his can also be ours, if in our hunger to be free we say no to sin and yes to God.

Now let's go on to see what living with sexual integrity can mean for us.

What the Bible says

2

The Bible has a lot to say about integrity in sexual matters; more than most people realize. But since the Bible means so little to so many, the truths it can focus on daily living are ignored. Our society is in turmoil from that ignorance.

How often do you think this kind of experience happens? A lovely young woman came to me one day for counsel. She worked for a married man and in the intimacies of long hours together, he presented himself as friend, companion, and finally, lover.

He seduced her. She fell in love. But instead of happiness, the woman felt increasing regret and guilt. When she came to see me, she was filled with despair and remorse.

Some of our famous (or is it simply notorious?) sex therapists might encourage the woman to enjoy her sexual opportunities and ignore the guilt. One or two might even say her problem is an over-reactive conscience resulting from strict parental pressures.

But isn't it time we had another look at the casual approach our society takes toward sex? This woman, for instance, is caught in a situation she now hates. She has little help from society in the struggle with her conscience. In fact, she has no substantial guidelines from society at all, except perhaps that if it feels good, enjoy it.

But that offers her no consolation now. She finds she is alone, more alone than she has ever been in her life. Her lover is false. He has a wife and family, which makes her guilt acute. She feels she has done irreparable damage to the man's other relationships.

Don't tell her she isn't responsible, that it's all his fault. She knows with her mind that he has been the aggressor in their affair. But that doesn't free her from her shame and self reproach. She knows that she could and should have avoided the mess she's in. Somehow.

She is right. There are too many instances where women are forced to consider an exchange of sex for job security, a pernicious form of rape.

But she can't forgive herself for falling into the trap. At this point, anyone who condemns her for an overactive conscience has seriously misunderstood human sensitivities, and wouldn't be much help to her in her pain.

If the Bible presents a clear understanding of human nature, and I among millions of others am convinced that it does, then we can benefit from its insight. In fact, one of the great purposes of the Bible is to reveal us to ourselves; to show us what we look like in contrast to what we could be, by the grace of God.

One of the most profound demands of the Bible concerns the place and function of sex. Yes, it is to take place exclusively in marriage. Yes, it is to produce children. But there is more. In the opening chapter of Genesis, we are created male and female and given the mandate to "Be fruitful and increase in number; fill the earth and subdue it." In the second chapter, woman is torn from man as if one flesh is pulled apart, so that man looks upon woman and says,

> "This is now bone of my bones
> and flesh of my flesh..."

"For this reason a man will leave his father and mother and be united to his wife, and they will become one flesh" (Genesis 2:23, 24).

These are the words Jesus repeated when some opponents were trying to prove his ideas about marriage were unorthodox. Jesus adds the well known phrases used in marriage ceremonies even today:

> "So they are no longer two but one.
> Therefore what God has joined together, let not man separate" (Matthew 19:6).

Until recently, this is how Christian marriage was perceived; a lifetime contract based upon the command of God. Vows were sacred. The commitment was irreversible.

Yet more is involved in marriage. A license is not enough. Even vows are not enough, in themselves. The bond that is represented by marriage, and which involves the sex act, is meant to be the beginning of a lifelong process of becoming one.

Sexual integrity in the Bible is based on this foundation. A man and a woman giving themselves to each other in marriage are doing something far more serious than begetting children in response to the command of God.

God has more for marriage than just children. His program for a couple involves their growing closer in friendship and companionship.

That is why a sexual incident *outside* of this relationship can only be destructive. And sex *before* marriage can only weaken the possibilities for a healthy growing bond later on. Similarly, kinds of sexual activity in marriage that are not mutually beneficial can only put a strain on the relationship.

Sexual images of faith

Sexual "purity" is a factor of considerable significance for a healthy marriage. Something remarkable occurs when two distinct personalities are knitted into one new entity, yet it can be damaged easily by sexual selfishness.

In fact, as far as the Bible is concerned, marriage and sexual fidelity are images used to describe the processes of genuine faith. In the Old Testament, faithfulness to the God of Abraham, Isaac and Jacob was often described in terms of marital fidelity.

God took his people as a husband takes a bride, "'I gave you my solemn oath and entered into a covenant with you,' declares the Sovereign Lord, 'and you became mine'" (Ezekiel 16:8).

Similar writings in the Old and New Testaments draw the parallel between sexual purity and the purity of true faith.

Without purity, faith has no meaning. In the Psalms, the writer asks,

"Who may ascend the hill of the Lord?
Who may stand in his holy place?
He who has clean hands and a pure heart,
who does not lift up his soul to an idol
or swear by what is false"(Psalm 24:3, 4).

Jesus echoes this in Matthew 5:8;

"Blessed are the pure in heart,

> for they will see God."

The writer of Hebrews makes the same point,

> "Make every effort to live in peace with all men and to be holy; without holiness no one will see the Lord" (Hebrews 12:14).

Holiness results from the commitment we make to live as God intended us to live. We trust him, follow the leading of his Holy Spirit in our lives, act in kindness and charity toward our neighbors and in the process become pure in heart.

The apostle Paul summed it up in his letter to the Christians at Ephesus:

> Be imitators of God, therefore, as dearly loved children and live a life of love, just as Christ loved us and gave himself for us as a fragrant offering and sacrifice to God.
> But among you there must not be even a hint of sexual immorality, or of any kind of impurity, or of greed, because these are improper for God's holy people (Ephesians 5:1-3).

Sex is a pure and holy thing in the marriage relationship. There is nothing shameful or sinful about sex when it functions in the role God ordained for it.

For us there are two ways to learn about sex outside of marriage. One is by experience, but that's the way of suffering and remorse. The second is by accepting the counsel of historical evidence. Throughout history and in virtually all cultures, sex outside of marriage has been destructive.

Sex in marriage is pure, normal, and important to the relationship. It is under the blessing of God.

Sex outside of marriage destroys the foundations for healthy relationships. It can be socially, psychologically and physically damaging.

I have never met a person, young or old, who

looked back with regret on a life of sexual fidelity. Purity brings no disappointment, leaves no remorse, and helps build a noble and worthwhile life.

"Here, then, is the message which we have heard from him: GOD IS LIGHT, and no shadow of darkness can exist in him. Consequently, if we were to say that we enjoyed fellowship with him and still went on living in darkness, we should be both telling and living a lie. But if we really are living in the same light in which he eternally exists, then we have true fellowship with each other, and the blood which his Son shed for us keeps us clean from all sin.

"If we refuse to admit that we are sinners, then we live in a world of illusion, and truth becomes a stranger to us. But if we freely admit that we have sinned, we find God reliable and just — he forgives our sin and makes us thoroughly clean from all that is evil" (First Letter of John 1:5-9, Phillips).

Judgment for impurity

3

In our society, we don't think about "judgment" very much, except for criminals. Ordinary people like you and me aren't criminals; we don't get into trouble with the law and so we have no worries about judgment. Or do we?

Most of us have heard about heaven and hell, and about God as a judge of our actions here on earth. And most of us have gone through some process of accommodation with this doctrine. Some reject the idea. Some accept it. Others don't quite know what to think and tend to ignore the subject.

I firmly believe in what the Bible teaches about heaven and hell, and the judgment of God. And one of the reasons I am certain of God's judgment is that I see it in action all around us today, just as the Bible described it.

This is going to be a tough chapter to read and digest, and maybe you'll feel like skipping its implications to get to the positive stuff later on. That's okay, feel free to do so. Just so you know that there *are* consequences for doing the wrong thing. Just as long as you know that cause and effect relationships do exist. Just as long as you come back sometime to see what the Bible has to say about sexual impurity.

Let's take an example. In the letter to the Hebrew Christians, the writer says, "Marriage should be honored by all, and the marriage bed kept pure, for God will judge the adulterer and all the sexually immoral" (Hebrews 13:4 NIV).

Now if the Biblical idea of purity was the other way around, so that marriage was the sin and sexual infidelity was the "right" thing to do, we might expect that God would bless infidelity and bring judgment on married love.

But that isn't the case. Throughout human history, fidelity in marriage has been the source of great happiness and contentment. And sexual experiences outside of marriage have brought a harvest of misery and remorse.

One of the great dramas in the Bible begins when David, King of Israel, looks out over Jerusalem from the roof of his palace. Below in the dusk he sees Bathsheba bathing in the seclusion of her garden, and is consumed with the desire to have sex with her.

Even though Bathsheba is married, King David has her brought to his bed. Later he discovers she is pregnant by him. Since her husband, Uriah, is fighting in the king's army, David has him brought home so he will sleep with Bathsheba and the child can be passed off as her husband's.

But David's plot backfires. Out of loyalty to his fellow soldiers who are still fighting and cannot sleep with their wives, Uriah refuses to go to Bathsheba. He sleeps in the palace on a mat in the servant's quarters.

David's passion for Bathsheba continues to

grow. After Uriah goes back to his unit, David orders his general, Joab, to put Uriah in the middle of the heaviest fighting to be sure he is killed. To honor David's request, Joab puts the whole unit in a battle, and a number of men are killed, including Uriah.

Bathsheba then becomes one more of David's wives. Even before this, jealousies between wives and children have begun. David's life is marked with endless turmoil. His favorite son Absalom attempts to tear the kingdom from him. Another son, Adonijah, sets himself up as king in David's place but loses out to Bathsheba's scheming for her son Solomon.

David may be one of the most striking persons of faith in the Old Testament, but from the time of his affair with Bathsheba his ability to govern Israel declines.

Sexual perversion

Under Old Testament law sexual immorality called for a penalty of death, whether for adultery or perversions. The classic case for God's judgment is Sodom and Gomorrha. The twin cities were destroyed by fire because of the perversion of the men there, who sought sexual relations with other men. That's where we get the word sodomy, describing anal sexual intercourse.

In the book of Leviticus, the law of God is outlined in considerable detail. Abnormal sexual relationships are expressly forbidden. In chapter 18 the lengthy list prohibits sex between mother and son, father and daughter, brother and sister, or any close relative. Sex with someone else's spouse brings dishonor, and to have sex with both a woman and her daughter "is wickedness."

"Do not lie with a man as one lies with a woman; that is detestable.

"Do not have sexual relations with an animal and defile yourself with it...that is a perversion....

"Everyone who does any of these detestable things—such persons must be cut off from their people....I am the Lord your God."

From the beginning the Bible has taught clearly that sexual relations are appropriate only between husband and wife, with all others declared wrong. Yet we have a lot of people today living as if it were right the other way around. Sex is "natural," we are told, and we do not need to be faithful to one spouse just because religion says so.

Sexual freedom

Some have argued that Jesus set us free from the law of God, as if to say we could go ahead and have sexual relationships any way we want to. But Jesus did not cancel the law of God; in fact, as he put it, he intended to add depth and scope to it, to fill it with meaning (Matthew 5:17-48).

In effect, Jesus moved morals to a higher level. The law said, Do not commit adultery. Jesus took it further—anyone who even looks at a woman lustfully has already committed adultery with her in his heart. There is much more to sex than just the physical, and we'll talk about that again in another chapter. But for now let's suppose that the law of God is also the law of nature. If that is true, then we could expect to find some data to support the idea.

A scientist would say that a law of nature gives evidence of its validity through the results you get from obeying the law, or breaking it. Jump off the

Empire State Building, and the laws of physics say you'll be going well over a hundred miles an hour when the sidewalk stops you. The validity of the law is demonstrable.

If then the law of God in sexual matters is also a law of nature, we can expect some evidence of its validity.

For instance, we can say by this law that, no matter how often a husband and wife have sex together, neither husband nor wife will ever become infected by a venereal disease. If they are virgins when they marry and remain faithful to each other, we can count on the law to work.

Turn the coin over and we can say sexually transmitted diseases give evidence that the law of God—and of nature—has been broken. Our civilization has chosen to ignore this law, and we have ample evidence of the results.

Sexually transmitted diseases

Chlamydia and gonnorrhea are the two most common sexually transmitted diseases today, afflicting nearly *six million* women each year. The findings were reported in the May, 1987 issue of the *Journal of the American Medical Association.*

This report advocates the use of contraceptive sponges by women in order to reduce the risk of contracting chlamydia. In a similar way, health officials encourage the use of condoms to avoid the transmission of AIDS. But neither Acquired Immune Deficiency Syndrome (AIDS) nor any other sexually transmitted disease would be as threatening to society if we accepted the law of God as the law of nature.

Promiscuous sex poses a severe threat to the

body's defenses. It is playing with fire and hoping not to get burned, yet in effect we're telling people to go ahead and take the risk.

No professional with a grain of common sense will argue that using heroin or cocaine is a safe way to enjoy life. Few will encourage young people to take up smoking, recommending abstinence instead. So why are our professionals so lax in warning people against the life-threatening risks of promiscuity?

Many become angry at the suggestion that AIDS or any other sexually transmitted disease is the "judgment of God." Yet one fact remains, no *sexually transmitted* disease is a threat to anyone who adheres to the law of God.

No one is under an obligation to believe in God's judgment, just as no one is obliged to live in obedience to the call and direction of God's spirit. Yet that does not change the reality of the law, certainly not in the case of sexually transmitted diseases. Break the law of God and the law of nature will impose its judgment, whether one believes in judgment or not.

Sexual myths

There is perhaps no time in our lives we are so blinded to reality as when our emotions and passions are stirred. Under sexual arousal people do more foolish things and throw their lives away more quickly than under any other circumstance.

So it pays to steer clear of situations that will lead to sexual arousal. Today that's not easy. We are conditioned to take sex lightly. Advertisements use sex to sell products. Television programs and movies feature sex, the more explicit the better. Novels are measured by the sexual details they include.

Women are often asked to perform sexually in order to keep a job. Girls at school soon get the message that to be popular with boys they must become sexually active.

These are the myths we are being asked to accept today (and some people don't believe in an evil force in the world!)

"Take suitable precautions. Use contraceptives. Enjoy." This is advice from the world, not from the Word of God.

Yet such advice has led to an epidemic of sexually oriented problems. Each day thousands of infants are born to unwed mothers, born without the father's commitment or care. Thousands of infant lives are aborted each day in what has been called the most common form of contraception, and the baby pays for the parent's selfishness with its life.

To use the prophet Hosea's memorable way of saying it, those who ignore the covenant God has made with his people "sow the wind, and reap the whirlwind."

But the grace of God is greater than our self-destructiveness, greater than our weakness, greater than all the power of evil to hide truth from us.

God gives his strength to those who ask for and accept it. There is only one requirement: that we sincerely desire to turn from our way of life to his. We provide the willingness; he provides the strength.

We can live on a new level if we turn our backs on sin. Let's face it, sexual activity outside God's covenant is sin. It brings severe judgments that cannot be avoided. If we don't accept that, we're fooling ourselves.

Sexual responsibility

4

It happened years ago, but I still remember the bitterness expressed in the small town when a young unmarried girl died of venereal disease. Suspicion and blame fell on the men who had taken her out. Gossip stained her friends and family.

Most of us gossip. News about other people can start a conversation quicker than anything else. And while much of it is relatively harmless, gossip can be devastating.

Sexual indiscretions still bring on the juiciest gossip. Today it may not be so unusual for teenagers to have sex, but be sure of this, kids know who is sexually active and who isn't.

But to go back to the young girl who died of a sexually transmitted disease, was she the worst sinner in town? Or was it the man who infected her, and didn't warn her of the danger?

What about the men who, relieved they never had sex with her or with anyone but their wives, have nevertheless enjoyed fantasies about sex with other women? Are they "better" somehow?

What about the women who tore her apart with

their tongues; were they so free of sin? Are sexual sins worse than gossip sins?

It cannot be wrong to feel good about yourself. People who hate themselves struggle with feelings of despair and futility. Life will never have much meaning for the man who is constantly putting himself down, for the woman who feels she is a failure.

However, it's wrong to hide one's capacity for evil from oneself. Most of us are capable of hurting other people as easily as we drink a cup of coffee. And simply because we hide our lust and hatred, envy and prejudice from outside view doesn't mean they're not there.

The Devil's strategy is to make people feel easy in their sins. But there is not one verse of scripture to tell us that immorality is worse when it is discovered out in the open than when it is hidden in the heart. Immorality indulged in secret is every bit as wrong as that done arrogantly where anyone can see it.

Yet it's a common thing for us to believe our secret immoralities are hidden from others. But we are only fooling ourselves, because what we are soon becomes apparent to others, and that includes the things we hide from view. "Character" is the word we give to the visible summing up of a person's life. And the evil shows up along with the good.

The apostle Paul wrote about it, "Remember that some men's sins are obvious, and are equally obviously bringing them to judgement. The sins of other men are not apparent, but are dogging them, nevertheless, under the surface. Similarly some virtues are plain to see, while others, though not at all conspicuous, will eventually make themselves felt" (1 Timothy 5: 24, 25, Phillips).

No one can outmaneuver that particular tenet of God's law. No one wins an argument with God over what is sinful in their life and what is not. The Bible says, "Do not be deceived: you cannot cheat God. A person reaps what he sows. The man who does what he pleases will grow a character to match; the man who plants according to the Spirit of God, from the Spirit will reap a life with eternal consequences written all over it" (Galatians 6:7, 8, author's paraphrase).

The decay of society

In this chapter we take the idea of consequences a step further than in the last chapter. One sign of the decay in our civilization is the indifferent attitude toward immorality of all kinds. History demonstrates that great nations collapse because of social corruption.

Moral decay brings an increase in crime, disintegration of home life, and a weakening of social structures. Sexual immorality adds its unique diseases, now approaching epidemic proportions. And we have hardly begun to understand the psychological devastation sexual impurity brings.

Rape is becoming more common. Pornography has crept out into the open, corrupting youngsters as well as adults. Children are molested at home, at school, in parks, on the playgrounds.

Erotic books on the newsstands try to make pleasures out of perversions. On television, some soap opera characters move through an unending sequence of lovers, bringing a new low to the meaning of fidelity in marriage.

What of marriage itself? Today most people seem to go into marriage with an eye for the nearest exit. No profession of fidelity has real meaning if it is qualified: "I will be faithful as long as this marriage meets my needs, but then I'm gone."

We are trying to change the laws of God's creation and the rules of human nature. We are denying that sin has a consequence. In effect, we are denying sin.

Karl Menninger, one of this century's leading psychiatrists, described the disappearance of morality in his best-seller, *Whatever Became of Sin?* (New York: Hawthorn Books, 1973).

Society's awareness of sin faded for a number of reasons, Menninger points out, one being the conversion of sin into crime and punishable by the courts. What had been the work of ministers and priests now came under the jurisdiction of lawyers and judges.

Other sins, according to Menninger, became the responsibility of doctors, psychiatrists and psychologists. Sin became sickness. Mental disorder. Psychological misbehavior. While there are valuable insights in each of these concepts, one result has been to dismiss a sense of personal responsibility for wrongdoing.

Yet this is what Menninger sees as our hope for the future: accepting personal responsibility for evil.

Understanding our situation

We need psychiatrists and psychologists to help us understand what makes us tick, why we have feelings of jealousy, envy, hatred, lust, pride. But we need to understand more about ourselves than science can ever tell us.

Spiritual insight allows us to see ourselves as God sees us. That's the value of the Bible for us.

And the Bible addresses sin very clearly.

Sexual morality goes beyond doing whatever feels good. Without moral guidelines, people fall back on feelings; what else is there to go on? Men and women, without a sense of sin, get into sexual intimacies only to discover much later that there *are* moral values involved. Too late. Especially if an "unwanted" child is conceived. Or a social disease is transmitted from one to the other.

Here is the real focus of sin: *our lack of responsibility for each other.* Sin not only hurts the sinner, *but always hurts someone else as well.*

Let's establish the fact that sex outside marriage lacks the intense commitment demanded by a lifelong relationship. So it's no surprise that sexual intimacies outside of marriage are much more selfish than we've been willing to admit. And selfishness can never escape being sin.

What about heavy petting and sexual fondling? Since the couple doesn't actually engage in the sex act, are they managing to avoid sin?

Somewhere here we need to talk about temptation. When most of us have trouble resisting a few extra calories at dinner, what is going to make us strong enough to resist the terrific demands of sexual arousal?

There's no sense in blaming God for having made us this way. God made us for good, not evil. It isn't God who is tempting us. As the Bible explains, "For God cannot be tempted by evil, nor does he tempt anyone; but each is tempted when, by his own evil desire, he is dragged away and enticed. Then, after desire has conceived, it gives birth to sin; and sin, when it is full-grown, gives birth to death" (James 1:13-15).

So waiting for marriage—old fashioned as that idea may seem—makes ultimate sense. There are plenty of ways to enjoy a deepening friendship without sex, and without heavy petting, as we'll talk about later.

As I suggested before, there's more to sin than the act. There is more to sexual impurity than becoming involved with someone outside the commitment of marriage. The way we think about sex is part of it too.

I want to be realistic here. People think about sex. It is the basis of a lot of poetry, music, novels and art. Much of that can be and is produced just for the sake of profit. A sexy book sells. But not every book includes sex just for the sake of becoming a best seller.

Sex is a great mystery, and people are fascinated by mystery. So not all thoughts about sex are evil, not by any means. But some are. *How* we think about sex makes the difference. How we think about anything makes the difference between good and evil; this is the heart of the Christian gospel.

Faith is a matter of attitudes-in-action; our thoughts, beliefs and perceptions about God and his reality, and how we act on them. It starts for us *inside,* in the heart and the spirit.

Jesus put it this way, "What comes out of a man makes him 'unclean.' For from within, out of men's hearts, come evil thoughts, sexual immorality, theft, murder, adultery, greed, malice, deceit, lewdness, envy, slander, arrogance and folly. All these evils come from inside and make a man 'unclean'" (Mark 7:20-23).

Look at that list again. Each act rises out of an

attitude of heart that is given over to evil. Each act is marked by intense selfishness — certainly *not* for the health and well-being of the other person. And that's why Jesus could sum up the essence of obedience to God and his law so briefly. He was asked by a teacher of the law, "Of all the commandments, which is the most important?"

"The most important one," answered Jesus, "is this: 'Hear, O Israel, the Lord our God, the Lord is one. Love the Lord your God with all your heart and with all your soul and with all your mind and with all your strength.' The second is this; 'Love your neighbor as yourself.' There is no commandment greater than these" (Mark 12:28-31).

How we think and act toward others is the one factor that shows the difference between good and evil, sin and not-sin. It puts all our thoughts and actions about sex on a far different level than before.

To turn life around and head it in the right direction takes a simple measure of faith. We believe that God *has* got the right sort of life in mind for us and wants us to have it. Then it's a matter of exercising that faith in how we think and act.

With the amount of wrong-thinking all of us do, we need all the guidance the Bible can give us. That's why the people of God pay so much attention to the Bible. By reading it they stand a better chance of understanding what God has in mind for humanity.

Further, the Spirit of God can then use the thoughts and concepts we've gained from the Bible to instruct us further. We can see with *his* eyes what we are like and what we can do to become more as he wants us to be.

Turning life around

5

If the choice is ours, then we are indeed free to choose another way than the life of integrity I have been writing about. God has given us that freedom. But in making our choices, we must accept responsibility for the outcomes.

The Bible takes a strong stand against sexual promiscuity, but we are not forced to share the Bible's point of view. We make a decision and take the consequences of belief or unbelief. That's our privilege.

Yet I want to be sure the consequences are clearly understood. The Biblical concept of free choice is an ancient one, going back thousands of years. Joshua called on his people to choose between God's way and any other, urging them to serve the Lord God.

"But if serving the Lord seems undesirable to you," Joshua challenged, "then choose for yourselves this day whom you will serve" (Joshua 24:15 NIV). Joshua saw the decision to be relatively simple; conform to the popular beliefs of the pagan communities around them, or accept the authority of the Lord.

For Joshua there was only one response: '... as

for me and my household, we will serve the Lord."

To Joshua, integrity began with living God's way. Not the way of any lesser god, but the Lord of the heavens and earth, whose way of life is righteous. And righteous living includes honest dealings with stranger as well as kinfolk, care of the poor and sickly, justice for the widow and orphan, and pure-mindedness in sexual matters. No lusting after another man's wife, because—as an old bit of wisdom puts it—the thought is father to the deed.

The apostle Paul talked about the benefits of choosing the way of God in his letters to early Christians. Spiritual power is made available to us to help us avoid doing the wrong thing at the wrong time. Temptation can't overwhelm us, as long as we don't want it to. We have all the power of God ready to help us do what is right at the right time.

Consider the Christians living in Corinth. This bustling center of world commerce became one of the largest cities in Greece, a seaport full of people from all parts of the Roman Empire. Bankers, business leaders, politicians, shipbuilders, commercial traders formed an elaborate social structure policed by the Greek system of justice. Yet barely below the surface, an underworld operated in the city. Trade in stolen goods and drugs was as well organized then as today. Male and female prostitutes—including children—were easily available to its citizens.

In the middle of this turbulent city, Paul offered a new resource for living a life of integrity. In a community with plentiful temptations to greed, power, and sexual exploitation in any combination of desires, Paul told of a new opportunity to a higher quality of life.

No matter how powerful a test you may face,

Paul declared, "No temptation has seized you except what is common to man. And God is faithful; he will not let you be tempted beyond what you can bear. But when you are tempted, he will also provide a way out so that you can stand up to it" (1 Corinthians 10:13, NIV).

There is a time to run from temptation and a time to stand up to it and say "No!" God will give you the guidance you need, *if* you are truly willing to do as he leads you. That's the key; recognizing that God is who he is, and being willing to let him be Lord of your life.

God let us see what integrity is like in the life of Jesus. Jesus was asked to do some difficult things in his short lifetime. He confronted the dishonesty and greed of the temple bankers in Jerusalem. He refused to allow a woman caught in adultery to be stoned to death by her self-righteous accusers; instead he asked her to begin a new life of faithful, responsible living.

Jesus called on his listeners to love their enemies, to treat them with patience and forgiveness. Then in the hours before his capture and trial, Jesus asked his friends to watch with him, to pray with him in his struggle with the meaning of that quality of love.

Jesus prayed, "My Father, if it be possible, let this cup pass from me, nevertheless, not as I will, but let your will be done" (Matthew 26:39, paraphrased). God demonstrated the overcoming power of his grace as he strengthened Jesus throughout the desperate hours of his trial and gave him the compassion to forgive his executioners.

The power of God stood behind the integrity of Jesus. Integrity is the quality of life the Bible describes as righteousness. The word is not easy to understand. Some cynics think righteousness makes a person "so heavenly minded he's no earthly good." Far from it. Integrity demands a commitment to tough-minded honesty. In today's world, honesty is too often replaced with expediency.

Integrity demands tough-minded love also. In today's world, a lot of things called love are no more than impostors for the real thing. Genuine love doesn't push for sexual satisfaction at the expense of another. When someone insists on making love because of a desire for sex, that person isn't "making love" at all but is attacking the other person's integrity. Seduction is an act of violence, not love.

Sexual restraint

Sexual restraint is part of integrity, just as it is part of tough-minded, caring love. Yet because sex is such a strong drive and copulation gives such intense pleasure, restraint isn't easy. Even now, when the epidemic of AIDS shows how dangerous unrestrained sex can be, it's apparent that sex drives are stronger than fears of catching the dread disease.

So some medical authorities have begun to advocate the use of condoms for "safe sex". The idea seems to be that if you are going to be sexually active, the use of a condom might help prevent the spread of AIDS. Thus if you have the disease, you won't pass it on; or if you haven't, you won't get it.

Unfortunately, the use of a condom presupposes the lack of trust between partners, and announces the passing nature of the relationship. In many situations, that's enough to inhibit persons from using condoms, and the AIDS virus moves along to another victim.

In every period of history there have been people

who scoff at the idea of a God who knows more about how they should live than they do. Among them today are many who proclaim their freedom from Biblical morality. They have declared their freedom to enjoy sex any way they wish.

Sexual exploitation

Sexual liberty isn't something we invented in the twentieth century. Human nature being what it is, sexual experimentation is as old as Adam and Eve and the serpent. The only thing new is how public we have become with our erotica.

Only in recent years has it been possible for anyone to rent a pornographic videotape at a neighborhood store. Only in recent years have movies at neighborhood theaters contained sexually explicit scenes. Only in recent years have magazines showing sexually suggestive material been sold in neighborhood stores.

Perhaps the psychologists and psychiatrists who say this is healthy are right. But it seems to me that only in these same recent years have so many teenagers become sexually active. And so many more girls in their early teens have faced the terrible decision of whether to terminate their pregnancies with an abortion. And never before have we faced such an epidemic of sexually transmitted diseases.

AIDS is only the most visible of a number of evils resulting from sexual promiscuity. The virus kills its victims quickly. Yet the lives of many more victims are ended abruptly each day through abortion.

Yes, I know there are other factors involved in the debate over abortion—the right of a woman to have control over her body being a major one. But somehow the life of the unborn must be taken into consideration too.

Let me tell you a story drawn from the many I have heard as a pastor and counselor. It is fiction in that no one will be able to identify the persons and families involved. It is truth in that it accurately depicts the hurts so many have felt.

A young woman of 15—I'll call her Janet—had sexual relations with her boyfriend regularly for over a year before she became pregnant. She had been on the Pill but it made her feel sick, and sometimes she skipped several days. Using a condom at those times seemed to spoil things for them, Janet recalls now.

The boy—I'll call him Peter—said that he loved her and would stand by her whatever she chose to do, but admitted that he wasn't ready to quit school and become a full time father. His parents didn't want him to get married. Janet's mother worked and didn't want to accept the responsibility of another child.

So Janet went through an abortion. At the time it seemed the only sensible thing to do.

Yet it has nearly destroyed her. She knows the fetus was alive when it was sucked from her womb, and she hears its voice in her nightmares. She is haunted by its cries in her mind. She dreams of what the child might have been, sees it as a toddler running to her with arms outstretched.

A psychiatrist has seen Janet several times and advises her parents that she needs continued professional care in order to help her through her depression. But Janet resents the idea of treatment. She is afraid the counseling will deprive her of the baby she has conceived in her mind.

She no longer sees Peter, because he doesn't understand her depth of feeling and resents the implications of guilt. She feels ten years, twenty years older than Peter; older in some ways even than her mother who never had an abortion, never thought of having an abortion, and didn't grow up in a time when abortion became the final form of birth control.

Janet scorns the love she once felt for Peter. She now hates the sex she enjoyed with him because she feels it betrayed her into the decision she says she will regret for the rest of her life.

The psychiatrist assures her that the intensity of her guilt will fade. Janet knows that other women have terminated their pregnancies without feeling the way she does. But she also knows there are some who share her anguish, and she is angry that no one warned her beforehand that she might feel she had killed her baby. And she is bitter toward a world that makes sex seem so harmless for young people like her.

A situation we share

We don't hear enough about the Janets in our society. We don't want their guilt to become ours, so we'd rather they keep it to themselves.

Yet what of our responsibility? Our world has said to the Janets that being sexually active is normal. Our scientists provide the birth control methods. Our courts say that abortion is acceptable. So what is it the Janets know that we don't?

In the Bible story Joshua found the world around a threat to his people's righteous living. Isn't that Janet's situation too? Our society encouraged her in a direction her heart and conscience now tell her was a terrible mistake

It's easy to urge Janet to forgive herself and get on with her life. But life is made up of past as well as future, history as well as possibility. We have to live with our mistakes.

As I said at the beginning of this chapter, I want to be sure the consequences of our actions are clearly understood. Sexual activity outside the lifelong commitment of marriage exposes us to risks far greater than our world has been willing to recognize; risks to the soul, heart and mind as well as to the body.

I want also to affirm the power of God to overcome the most devastating temptations we face, whether temptations of mind or body or spirit.

In his letter to the Roman Christians, the apostle Paul confessed his struggles in life:

> I often find that I have the will to do good, but not the power. That is, I don't accomplish the good I set out to do, and the evil I don't really want to do I find I am always doing. Yet if I do things that I don't really want to do then it is not, I repeat, "I" who do them, but the sin which has made its home within me.... In my mind I am God's willing servant, but in my nature I am bound fast, as I say, to the law of sin and death. It is an agonizing situation, and who on earth can set me free from the clutches of my own sinful nature? I thank God there *is* a way out through Jesus Christ our Lord.
>
> No condemnation now hangs over the head of those who are "in" Christ Jesus. For the new spiritual principle of life "in" Christ Jesus lifts [us] out of the old vicious circle of sin and death ... so long as we are living no longer by the dictates of our sinful nature, but in obedi-

ence to the promptings of the Spirit... So then ... you can see that we have no particular reason to feel grateful to our sensual nature, or to live life on the level of the instincts. Indeed that way of living leads to certain spiritual death. But if then you cut the nerve of your instinctive actions by obeying the Spirit, you are on the way to real living....

The Spirit of God ... helps us in our present limitations. For example, we do not know how to pray ... but his Spirit within us is actually praying for us in those agonizing longings which never find words. And God who knows the heart's secrets understands, of course, the Spirit's intention as he prays for those who love God....

In the face of all this, what is there left to say? If God is for us, who can be against us? He who did not hesitate to spare his own Son but gave him up for us all — can we not trust such a God to give us, with him, everything else that we can need? (excerpts from Romans 7:18-8:32, Phillips).

God *is* on our side. He will forgive us and give us all the resources we need to survive temptation. All that is required of us is to commit ourselves to him and obey the promptings of his Spirit.

The rewards of integrity

6

When people think of rewards, it's usually in terms of cash. Wages for work. Professional fees. Royalties. Winning a sweepstakes. Hitting it big on the stock market.

Then there are fringe benefits; vacations with pay, health insurance, maternity/paternity leave, retirement funds.

And think how good it feels when a neighbor thanks you for babysitting in an emergency, or for providing transportation after a car breaks down.

So rewards can come in a variety of ways beside cash. In fact, the greatest rewards can't be measured in dollars and cents. To receive the faithful love of a cherished spouse is priceless. The last segment of the Book of Proverbs describes a wife of noble character:

> She is worth far more than rubies.
> Her husband has full confidence in her
> and lacks nothing of value.
> She brings him good, not harm,
> all the days of her life. (Proverbs 31:10-12, NIV).

Thus the writer closes the book of Proverbs, talking about the integrity of a woman who serves the Lord obediently and reverently—in effect, a woman who "fears" the Lord .

The book opens in a parallel way, by saying "The fear of the Lord is the beginning of knowledge; moral fools despise wisdom and discipline" (Proverbs 1:7, paraphrased). Note the other similarities:

> Blessed is the man who finds wisdom,
> the man who gains understanding,
> for she is more profitable than silver
> and yields better returns than gold.
> She is more precious than rubies;
> nothing you can desire can compare with her,
> Long life is in her right hand,
> in her left hand are riches and honor.
> Her ways are pleasant ways,
> and all her paths are peace (Proverbs 3:13-17, NIV).

The potential is there for everyone, male and female. Integrity brings its own blessings: satisfaction, peace of mind, contentment, respect, confidence in oneself as the fruit of confidence in the Lord God. God desires that all people should drink deeply of these blessings as a foretaste of eternal life, but he will not force them on anyone.

The person who doesn't care for integrity has no substance in life, no focus for trustworthiness, no basis for respect. He or she may achieve wealth and power, and even some measure of respect from those to whom wealth and power are important. But these "blessings" are not of God, since they are achieved at the expense of others.

Of course, how we go after our life goals in all ways affects others. If we ignore the needs of others in order to get to where we think we must go, we may wind up powerful and rich—or we may not. Being selfish holds no guarantee of fame and fortune.

Moving to integrity

Loving God with all the heart, mind, soul, and strength may not yield clout and a fat bank account either. But when combined with loving others as well as ourselves, *it does bring integrity.* And integrity is an essential element in what the Bible calls righteousness, a virtue more precious than rubies.

Righteousness begins with faith in God and obedience to his Spirit. That's not as difficult as it sounds, because God inspires the faith, then strengthens our willingness to respond to his will. When we do respond, he creates the climate for integrity to grow.

This process was outlined by Paul in his letter to the Christians in Rome. Faith straightens out and justifies our relationship with God, so that even in difficult circumstances we can rejoice, because difficulty produces perseverance in us, perseverance produces character, and character yields hope. And all of this is possible because God has "poured out his love into our hearts by the Holy Spirit, whom he has given us" (Romans 5:1-5, NIV).

In other words, we are *not* alone, we are *never* alone. God is *always* at work to bring us to faith in him. And with even the smallest response of faith from us—as small as a grain of mustard seed—he pours his resources into our lives, generously and abundantly.

That is why it's possible to stand up to temptations of any kind, even the most powerful sexual persuasions. God's spirit helps us in our weaknesses, so that even though we don't know how to pray for help, the Spirit within us communicates clearly with God. And God knows exactly what we need because he knows us better than we know ourselves (see Romans 8: 26, 27).

There's a distinct contrast between a life integrated with God and one that doesn't pay any attention to God's Spirit but lives to satisfy the desires of the lower nature.

> For the whole energy of the lower nature is set against the Spirit, while the whole power of the Spirit is contrary to the lower nature.... The activities of the lower nature are obvious. Here is a list: sexual immorality, impurity of mind, sensuality, worship of false gods, witchcraft, hatred, quarreling, jealousy, bad temper, rivalry, factions, party spirit, envy, drunkenness, orgies and things like that. I solemnly assure you, as I did before, that those who indulge in such things will never inherit God's kingdom. The Spirit, however, produces in human life fruits such as these: love, joy, peace, patience, kindness, generosity, fidelity, tolerance and self control — and no law exists against any of them.
>
> Those who belong to Christ Jesus have crucified their old nature with all that it loved and lusted for. If our lives are centered in the Spirit, let us be guided by the Spirit. (Galatians 5:17-25, Phillips).

As I have said before, the choice is ours. We can choose moral integration or moral disintegration. If we choose the latter, the world will give us all the help we need to lose our way morally. If we choose the righteousness of God, we have the enormous help of his Spirit, as close to us as our own spirit.

Does that mean we will never fall to temptation? Or that if we do fall, God won't help us again? Not at all. Remember, integrity is something that is built like a strong house on a solid foundation, brick by brick, joist by joist, nail by nail. Sometimes we may crack a brick, split a joist or lose a nail, but we don't stop building. We try to correct the mistakes we make and go on.

If our foundation is Jesus Christ, and if, as he counseled, we seek *first* "the kingdom of God and his righteousness" (Matthew 6: 33), we will discover how infinitely satisfactory is his care.

New perspectives

With faith in God, obedience to his Spirit, and a hunger for his integrity, here are a few of the things we can expect to achieve:–

1. *A clearer perspective on right and wrong.*

Until we begin living first for God's kingdom, we can't see moral issues with the right perspective. We see with eyes clouded by the ads and commercials of the world. "Kingdom" is a strange word to use in modern times; we don't have many kingdoms left. But God is more than a king or president or premier of a democracy—so much more. And his morality goes far beyond the morality of any culture or social structure. He *demands* love of enemy, but we allow ourselves to hate some neighbors, some nations. God *demands* justice for the poor; we argue about welfare reform.

2. *A new understanding of who we are.*

We are meant to be God's people, living with his kind of integrity. According to Jesus, if we cooperate with the spirit of God, we can accomplish great things, greater than we can imagine.

> "I tell you truly, anyone who believes in me will do what I have been doing and more, because I go to my Father — he is your Father too — and we will send the same Spirit, the spirit of truth that the world cannot receive because it doesn't recognize him" (John 14: 12-17, author's condensed paraphrase).

In effect, we have an active task to fulfill in God's kingdom. In a world menaced with hatred, mistrust, greed, immoralities, violence, sectarian jealousies and suspicions, we are to be strong stabilizing influences for love, justice, forgiveness, peace, humility, kindness, hope and morality.

3. *A new sense of responsibility for others.*

There is little doubt that everything we do has an influence on someone else, for good or ill. Let me tell you a story to illustrate what I'm getting at.

Tom was little more than a boy himself when his own boy was born. He lived with middle class parents in a major regional city. He met his girlfriend at high school during their senior year and a passionate relationship quickly developed. Evie lived with her parents a few blocks away, and they spent as much time together as school hours would allow.

Both were reasonably "good" kids and tried to go

no further than "heavy" petting. Then one night, prolonged genital fondling led to full intercourse.

The experience shook them both. It wasn't so much the physical impact of it, but something more profound seemed to be involved. For several dates, they avoided intimacy. Then, as if by mutual consent, they spent an afternoon in Evie's bed.

So far, this is the story of thousands of kids in our schools. Evie was an only child and both her parents had good paying jobs. Tom's folks wanted a large family, and with nine children his mother had her hands full keeping the household running smoothly. Again, not much different than the family pattern of thousands of other teenagers.

But both sets of parents were active Christians (note: being a Christian parent doesn't mean your children will be free of the problems of growing up), and had made a serious attempt to instill Christian values in Evie and Tom. Because of these teachings, Tom and Evie realized they were over their heads in a situation far deeper than anything they had ever been in before.

Next day, after a long, whispered discussion in the school library they acknowledged to each other how seriously they were violating their parents trust as well as their values. So Evie and Tom decided to tell their parents about their love for each other and confess their sexual activity. And here is where their story becomes unique.

At first, Evie's parents exploded in indignation and grounded Evie for the rest of the year. They prohibited her from seeing Tom ever again, and Evie cried herself to sleep that night.

Tom didn't fare much better. His father told him he was an irresponsible fool driven by his sexual hungers, and did he realize the position he had put Evie in with her family? Was he aware he had jeopardized his own future? Was he willing to accept the responsibility of parenthood while still in highschool? Tom spent most of that night staring at the ceiling.

In the morning, Evie's parents asked Tom's folks if they could come over that evening to talk. It was one of the longest days in Tom's life, yet when the two families met that night he asked to be the first to speak.

He spoke to Evie's parents first, asking them to realize Evie could have kept silent but that out of respect she had chosen to tell her parents what was happening. He explained he wanted his parents to know for the same reason, and that he and Evie were asking for help. They loved each other and wanted to get married as soon as possible.

As the parents hesitated, Evie asked to speak. With tears running down her cheeks, she pointed out that in most times in history—and in most cultures—she would likely have been married for several years and had children. But now she and Tom and all the others in their generation were being asked to prepare for careers first, while putting their need for love and companionship on hold.

To me the story of Tom and Evie stands out in three ways. First, they acknowledged the Christian values of their parents. Second, they accepted the responsibility of their failure to live up to those ideals and confessed to their parents and to God. And finally, Tom and Evie asked for help.

As it turned out, Evie was pregnant. Their parents helped them get married, and they are trying to carve out a life for themselves and their little boy. Their struggle has not been easy, and they have grown to appreciate the values of their parent, because now they are parents too.

Most sexually active young people don't want to think about any values that might conflict with their own. Most parents refuse to accept any responsibility for the changed values in society that make it so difficult for children today. And neither parents nor young people know any better way to deal with the change in morals.

This book recommends a new-old approach to cover a number of different situations. It takes its counsel from the Bible and from the Christian values of the church. Now in the remaining chapters, let's see how those values can be adapted to meet some of the situations our society imposes upon us today.

Life without sex?

7

For some people, living without sex is a contradiction in terms; life *is* sex, and life without sex for them cannot be called life. It is true that some persons seem to have a higher sex drive than others. But, like every appetite common to humankind, our sex drive can be controlled. Which means it is possible to live without sex.

I'm not saying it's easy to do. But I can tell you a number of reasons why it's worth considering.

1. AIDS is only one reason. There are 37 other sexually transmitted diseases to look out for, including some strains that have become resistant to available antibiotics.

2. Parenthood permanently changes the lives of those involved; ask any woman who has ever borne a child. With new laws attempting to force financial responsibility upon fathers, even the man who takes his sexual activity lightly may feel the weight.

3. We have no way to measure the psychological

cost of abortion on the mother or the father, but some evidence is beginning to accumulate that points to a permanent effect. For some it's guilt. A few seem untouched by the death of the fetus—I would say they are hardened. For others the feelings are ambiguous. But no one who has gone through the experience is ever quite the same.

These are all negative reasons for doing without sex. There are positives too:

4. You control your body, it doesn't control you. Glandular drives are strong. Yet with God's help you can master your sexual impulses. Saint Paul talked about his struggles often, but in his letter to the Christians at Corinth he spoke of the rewards of self control — it verified his life and his ministry (1 Corinthians 9:26, 27).

5. You will know your full capabilities, unscrambled by the fierce emotions and complications sex outside of marriage can bring to your life.

6. When you find the person you want to spend the rest of your life with, you can bring to that relationship your unblemished loyalty.

7. With sex in its proper perspective you can see the other attractive qualities of character in the person you are drawn to marry. Don't take my word for it alone. There are millions of successful marriages out there, and I guarantee you that in every one, sex is only one of a number of compatabilities.

Marriage is the closest, most demanding relationship you'll ever have, and you need to *like* the person you marry as well as love them. To do that, you need to explore how you feel about a lot of other characteristics before sex blurs your vision.

Lifelong relationship

Maybe this sounds a little cold-hearted and unromantic to you. If it does, I'm sorry, I don't mean it that way at all. Romance is the spice of life; notice, I said romance, not sex. There's a huge difference. In today's world, some people want to make sex as casual a recreation as bicycling or golf. In doing so the integrity of a romantic relationship is threatened; I can't think of anything more cold-hearted than sex without romance.

There is nothing more natural and normal than for those of the opposite sex to be attracted to each other. We are made that way. It is not only a biological reality; affinity has its affirmation in the spirit as well. For the mates who have woven their love together in total commitment, life isn't long enough.

A friend told me a story that illustrates the depth of affinity in a bittersweet way. The story was picked up and carried by the national news media and involved a pair of black mallard ducks, who mate for life.

My friend and some of his cronies were duck hunting on a pond in southern Ontario. It was opening day of the season and the pond had more than its share of hunters. "There were more hunters than ducks," Glen recalls.

"Even though they were old enough to have been through a season or two, those black mallards didn't have a chance.

"They were cautious, flying in high over the pond, but someone out in the reeds hit the hen with a long shot and she tumbled into the water.

"I've never seen anything like it, and I hope I never see it again," Glen says. "The drake swung wide over the fields west of the pond then came back, looking for his mate.

"Most of the hunters on the pond couldn't have hit a barn with a shovel standing next to it. But the drake didn't know that. Before he got close enough to reach, some hunters began to fire. The drake kept coming, homing straight in on where the hen fell.

"He took several pellets from a couple of near misses—you could see him stumble in the air a little—but he sifted in, calling to her all the way. I don't know how he got as close to her as he did before he took the full charge that killed him."

Glen says he rediscovered something about loyalty and commitment that day, his last day of hunting. "Don't take me wrong, I won't fault someone else for hunting. I just wouldn't be able to lift my gun anymore without seeing that drake coming in like he did.

"He knew something was wrong. He didn't care about himself, he just wanted to be with his downed mate."

A matter of integrity

Sex for recreation cannot produce loyalty and caring. Yet sex is meant to be the bonding joy of a life commitment. So it seems to me that sexual activity apart from commitment is certain to weaken any capacity we have for loyal bonding. I am convinced we owe the high rate of divorce today to our weakened ability for commitment.

Because we aren't willing to live without sex until we can commit ourselves to a lifetime spouse, we cannot hold that commitment when we make it.

"But," you may ask, "what if I don't find the one for me? It happens all the time. Lot's of people don't find a mate. Am I supposed to give up sex for the rest of my life?"

Why not? How can you be sure you won't find your beloved tomorrow, or next week, or next year? That happens all the time too.

And the longer you retain your integrity, the more you will bring to your marriage.

Help for saying no

Living without sex starts with the help of the Holy Spirit. Don't let the word "Holy" put you off. The term is reverential as well as practical; we use it to express our feelings of gratitude as well as describe the quality of that presence in our lives.

There is a lot to the meaning of the word, but for our purposes let's focus on *wholeness*. God is complete, integrated, *and he brings with him the spirit of integrated wholeness*. When you take the step of putting your life in his hands, submitting your spirit to his Spirit, you are in fact setting your life on God's track of integrated wholeness.

The choices you face will always have several alternatives, but only one will lead in the direction of integrated wholeness. Only one will be the way of the *Holy* Spirit. It is often the tough choice. If it were the easy way, the world would be a lot nicer place in which to live. It isn't, simply because enough people enough of the time make choices apart from integrity. Not only criminal choices—although there is a great deal of underworld behavior going on around us—but just plain selfish choices as well.

Sexual activity is very often the most selfish thing we do. We gratify the terrific urge to copulate.

And while it would be nice if the partner were good looking, healthy, admiring, and grateful, a lot of times it's just the willingness of the sex partner to participate that counts. It may be called "making love," but there's little love involved.

So the choice you make to wait for the one you can love for the rest of your life in marriage will put you in line for the strengthening of the *Holy* Spirit. You'll need his strength. The sex drive is powerful, and may push you to choose anyone who is handy.

A song rose out of the "free" love era of the '60s that goes something like this:–

> If you can't be with the one you love
> Love the one you're with.

Don't believe it. That is *not* love. One of the major themes of our world is that love and sex are the same thing; if you feel sexually attracted to a person, you can "make love" together. No, all you will be doing is having sex with each other. *And you will be diminishing your ability to actually love anyone but yourself.*

I can't say it often enough: love depends on the wholeness of intent and the integrity of your concern toward the other person. In love, you want the best for the other person, not the fulfillment of your own sexual desire.

The Spirit of Holy wholeness will help you be loving without expecting to have sex. That brings up what I call psychological rape: "If you loved me, you'd have sex with me." If you have been tempted to use this old threat, realize that's exactly what it is, a not-so-subtle form of extortion. If you do use it, you have lost all right to the love you're exploiting.

The question of masturbation

If it's possible to live without sex, what about masturbation? If we believe the psychologists, the curiosity we have about ourselves leads to exploration of the genitals and to orgasms brought on by self-manipulation. Some argue that this is healthy—at least healthier than premarital or extra-marital sex.

Others insist that sexual love is only best expressed in marriage; anything less than that diminishes our ability to give love to the beloved, therefore acts of masturbation are inappropriate. In marriage it is a form of mental adultery; before marriage it overemphasizes sexual satisfaction.

Still others believe that, until marriage, masturbation is the lesser of several evils, all other evils involving someone else and bringing them harm as well as ourselves. This view sees auto-eroticism as release of sexual tension that might otherwise be harmful.

As we have seen, the Bible is very outspoken on sexual acts which involve someone else. It has little to say about masturbation; the one reference most commonly cited is the story of Onan, in Genesis 38. However this account tells of family intrigue and irresponsibility, and has nothing to do with autoeroticism.

Here again I must honor the Spirit of wholeness, who leads us towards integrity from wherever we are when we commit ourselves—for the first or the forty-first time—to living his way. We'll come up against all manner of choices in life that we won't find discussed in the Bible. But we will find principles to guide us in its pages.

Saint Paul pointed out that in such matters he found the basic answer lies in the effect our action will have upon others. What our conscience allows us to do as we live in harmony with the Holy Spirit is quite appropriate. But if what we do becomes an offense to someone else, or diminishes our relationship in any way, we should not do it (see I Corinthians 8).

We can live without sex by diverting our attention from it—again, not an easy task in our overly stimulating world. But there are so many wonderful things out there to do, there is no reason why we can't find plenty of release for our energies.

We don't have to deny our sexuality in order to live without sex. Our sexual natures aren't just expressed in genital activity, not by any means. Many persons who live without sex are intensely sexual beings. Femininity and masculinity, when directed by the Holy Spirit, can be powerful forces for good in the world.

Thousands of people, young and old, go into voluntary service every year, giving of their energies in the most loving way to people in desperate need. Many religious denominations have volunteer services, and there are agencies of the government in most Western nations for volunteer work in developing countries.

And that's only one very obvious possibility for channeling your sexuality in service to others.Living without sex can free you for a lot of loving in a lot of ways.

Living with integrity opens the door to friendship with the finest people in the world. Look around you today, chances are the ones who are doing great things are those who have channeled their sexuality into caring about the world and the people in it.

Courting for marriage

8

I would like us to get our terms straight. Courting is an old fashioned term we don't hear a lot about these days, but it will help to revive it for the sake of contrast. Dating, as a friend calls it, is "kicking tires," shopping for the kind of person you could get serious about.

If you are dating, you're still hunting the one you want to spend the rest of your life with. At least, that's the idea. On the other hand, courting is dating with a more serious purpose, to see if you are suited for a lifetime commitment.

I think most dating couples know when their interest in each other moves to a deeper level. It's the most normal thing in the world to look forward to a happy married relationship. The Bible encourages people to get married, "He who finds a wife finds what is good and receives favor from the Lord," (Proverbs 18:22).

In its second chapter, Genesis tells how the Lord God tore woman out of the flesh of man so that when joined together in marriage, husband and wife can return to a state of completeness and become as if they were "one flesh."

There are few things more important than starting marriage on the right note. So what you do on the level of dating and courting becomes vital. Integrity isn't something to turn on and off like a flashlight. It is the substance of a person's character and involves the ideals and standards we bring to everything we do.

If we take our lead from television and videocassettes, we're going to be disappointed. Some stories show what a healthy marriage can be like, but for every good movie relationship there seems to be a dozen or more suffering from terminal superficiality.

Perhaps it's because good relationships don't make for interesting drama. A novel without several episodes of illicit sex isn't likely to be a best seller—at least that is what we've been taught to expect.

But what makes for dramatic entertainment isn't what you should take as an example of reality. For one thing, all those gossipy divorces are pretty rough in real life. Long, bitter struggles, with lawyers taking a big bite out of your pocketbook; children devastated by guilt, wondering what they did to cause the split; years of opportunity to develop marriage skills forever wasted on failure.

So what we do in dating and courting has immediate value. The Bible is clear; no part of life is unrelated to the whole. Let's look at some of its guidelines.

1. *Consider dating and courting part of your spiritual experience.*

Body, mind, soul and spirit, we belong to God; he has a claim on our lives by every good experience that moves us toward spiritual integrity. What we do on a date can either strengthen us spiritually or make us weaker. Most of us are so caught up with the physical aspects, we don't work on our spiritual vitality. We haven't as yet understood how necessary the life of the spirit is to us individually.

What is more, we are collectively interconnected, so that the person we date is part of us too. In a very real sense, we are God's building, together.

2. *Set your standards and ideals before you begin dating.*

There's an enormous difference between integrity and *dis*-integrity; between the wholesome and the unholy. We can't put life in separate compartments, be a *little* honest, *occasionally* loyal, *sometimes* faithful.

If you really are committed to a life of "righteousness, peace and joy in the Holy Spirit," you will establish your standards of conduct *before* you go on a date. Then you'll find it easier to reject situations that may lead to sexual activity.

Don't be afraid to stand by your standards, especially when you're tempted to let down. Remember this, intimacies on a date can pull you into emotional arousal. Sexual desire can get to be tremendously demanding if you let it diminish your control. So don't lose control. Establish that ahead of time. Give your body—as well as your mind and spirit—to God in unreserved commitment.

This is what being a Christian is all about, nothing less, as the apostle Paul wrote :

"I urge you by God's mercy to offer your bodies to him as a living gift of worship, dedicated and fit for his acceptance, the appropriate worship of an intelligent mind. Do not let the world form you in its pattern but let your minds be transformed so that you know the will of God by knowing what is good and acceptable and perfect" (Romans 12: 1, 2, author's paraphrase).

With that kind of Christian commitment you can retain control on your dates. You won't be embarrassed to suggest activities that are fun and interesting and that won't lead to the back seat of a car, or to a bed in someone's apartment.

You won't cut yourself off from others when you date. Plan skating with some friends. Play volleyball together. Get into a Christian activity group, so you have a chance to mix with people whose ideals are being pulled in the right direction.

Introduce your date to your family, so that you can share in family events—picnics, reunions, birthday parties. Seeing your date in the context of family celebrations will tell you a lot about the person you won't find out in any other way.

Go biking. Visit the zoo. Stroll the mall just to watch people go by. Take in a concert. Do a jigsaw puzzle.

Attend church together. Pray together. Talk about your faith together. If your date can't share your Christian commitment, you can expect much more serious differences to show up later. That's my next point.

3. *Expect Christian ideals in the person you date.*

You won't always be able to tell ahead of time what the person you date is really like. But don't compromise your ideals. Expect integrity and honesty; if you don't, you're apt to take anything that walks on two legs and breathes.

Young people worry about being accepted by their peers at school and can let themselves get talked into a sexual situation just to "belong." Older singles worry about missing out on intimacy altogether, and lower their standards in order to win a lover.

Let's look at this again from the perspective of faith. Jesus urged people to believe God cares about everything in their lives. If we worry and try to make God do things the way we think they should be done, we're going to miss the best.

Instead, if we put ourselves in God's hands, and look first for his way, then the best for us will be added to our lives as we go on trusting God (Matthew 6: 25-34).

Dating is a risky business, but it's the only way we have in our society of bringing together a man and a woman to see if they like each other enough to survive the intensity of marriage. Note that I said like, not love. Love can be blind to serious faults. You need to love the person you marry. But you must like your mate-to-be too.

Dating gives you an opportunity to study at close range the attitudes, conduct, capabilities and true worth of the person you're attracted to. You can't be sure ahead of time how the person you marry will act under certain circumstances. We know nothing of the future behavior of those we propose to wed; we must decide only on the basis of how they live and act now.

In most communities you would be wise to limit your dating to persons of your own religious persuasion. At college, students tend to ignore such guidelines because professors often criticize denominationalism as narrow and bigoted. This can be true, but on the practical level we need to live with the reality of denominations and their demands.

The focused intensity of marriage can survive differences of opinion on matters of faith, but not easily. It is wise to give God a chance to put you together with a person who appreciates the same religious beliefs and practices as you do.

Unfortunately, it is not necessarily safe to marry someone just because he or she is a member of your church. A young married woman once came to my wife and me for help. She was very unhappy in her marriage. She found her love worn thin, and life was almost unbearable at times.

She had married an active worker in her own denomination. Now he was cold spiritually and his behavior untrustworthy.

I don't remember all we talked of that night, but one thing I have never forgotten. She said that before they were married he bought things forbidden by his parents and kept them at her house. He was living a lie before his father and mother, and she knew it.

Perhaps she felt a lying son could become an honest husband. A lot of people have made the mistake of hoping to change the person they want to marry. Don't count on it. It could be the most unhappy mistake of your life.

While you are courting is the time to discover the reality of your friend's Christian experience, and to demonstrate the integrity of your own. *Never* count on reshaping the other person into the image of your dreams; life doesn't work that way. When people try to change other people they are playing God; a dangerous occupation for anybody without the necessary qualifications.

There is really only one safe procedure in the dating game:

4. *Put your life in God's hands, let him lead you in all your relationships.*

Where, among all the millions of people out there, is the person who can bless your life with love, friendship, loyalty and joy? How can you find the one you can love wholeheartedly for the rest of your days?

A friend of mine tells how he found his wife on a blind date. "When she opened the door," Tom says, " I was smitten right then and there.

"I know it isn't the wisest thing to accept love at first sight, but looking back now I know that God led me to her just as surely as I know the sun will come up tomorrow.

"I had dated a number of girls, but nothing ever clicked. I wasn't paying much attention to God at the time, I just figured he was around somewhere, looking after things. He sure was.

"We didn't know anything about each other then, and even now, after forty years, we're still finding out new things. She is my closest friend and confidant. I'll always be grateful to God for bringing us together."

One of their favorite parts of the Bible is found in Proverbs:

> My son, do not forget my teaching,
> but keep my commands in your heart,
> For they will prolong your life many years
> and bring you prosperity.
>
> Let love and faithfulness never leave you;

bind them around your neck,
Then you will win favor and a good name
in the sight of God and man.

Trust in the Lord with all your heart,
and lean not on your own understanding;
in all your ways acknowledge him,
and he will make your paths straight.

Do not be wise in your own eyes;
fear the Lord and shun evil.
This will bring health to your body
and nourishment to your bones (Proverbs 3: 1-8, NIV).

When people lean on their own mental processes, their own understanding about life, they miss out on the depth of insight God can provide. If you are not paying attention to his signals, you're not going to follow where he leads you.

But if you commit yourself to the Lord, he will direct your life. In thousands of circumstances, God will give you opportunity to follow him into a future of maturing faith.

How to know when God is leading

How can you know God is leading you in your decisions? A number of years ago I learned a seven step outline I've found very helpful.

1. Trust God with all your heart, mind, soul and strength. Let this trust be expressed in generous compassion for all of God's creation.

2. Study the scriptures, both Old and New Testaments. Hide the word of God in your heart so that

God has something in you to bring to mind in any situation in life. You have a conscience; make sure it is continually illuminated with Christ's teachings.

3. *Pray about your decisions.* In addition, cultivate an attitude of continual prayer, an openness to communication through the spirit of God. As Paul advised the Christians at Thessalonica, "Be joyful always; pray continually; give thanks in all circumstances, for this is God's will for you in Christ Jesus."

4. *Meet regularly with God's people* so you can receive the counsel of the body of Christ of which you are a member. "Just as each of us has one body with many members, and these members do not all have the same function, so in Christ we who are many form one body, and each member belongs to all others" (Romans 12: 4, 5, NIV).

5. *Take steps of faith in the choices you face.* Believe God is leading you, and move ahead with what appears as the *holy* choice. Your choices and actions will take into consideration the spiritual encouragement of others, and not be a stumbling block (see Romans 14).

6. *Expect the peace of God to affirm your decision.* If you are following the Spirit of God, you will enjoy "the peace that passes understanding." If you feel uncomfortable about your decision, it may be that you have made the wrong choice — or it may simply mean there is some fine tuning to be done before you will be content.

7. Be ready to revise and adjust to new input. Don't expect life to be composed of only one or two major decisions on which you consult God. The life of faith is total. Everything we do is done properly only as we follow the Holy Spirit, and his guidance is as intricate and complex as the problems we face daily.

> Those who live according to the sinful nature have their minds set on what that nature desires; but those who live in accordance with the Spirit have their minds set on what the Spirit desires. The mind of sinful man is death, but the mind controlled by the Spirit is life and peace; the sinful mind is hostile to God. It does not submit to God's law, nor can it do so. Those controlled by the sinful nature cannot please God.
>
> You, however, are controlled not by the sinful nature but by the Spirit, if the Spirit of God lives in you (Romans 8: 5-9, NIV).

Are you in love?

9

What is love? I have never heard anyone describe it satisfactorily. Those who say they are in love cannot find words adequate to their feelings. Yet love is real; it is thrilling, powerful, demanding, life-changing.

There are no love-meters to measure its intensity. Love is one of life's intangibles; the human race could not survive without it—

For love is as strong as death,
its jealousy unyielding as the grave.
It burns like blazing fire,
like a mighty flame.
Many waters cannot quench love;
rivers cannot wash it away.
If one were to give
all the wealth of his house for love,
it would be utterly scorned (Song of Songs 8: 6, 7 NIV).

Although it's impossible to define, love is a necessity for happiness in marriage. I urge you, do not get married unless you are *truly* in love!

A survey of the lovelife of five hundred college women found they had averaged five infatuations between the ages of twelve and eighteen. You can believe that each one felt like the real thing at the time.

I have a book in my library by Evelyn Millis Duval called *Facts of Life and Love* . She tells a story:

> Edith had to sit on Chris' lap in the car in which they both were driving home with several others from a school party. She had never paid any attention to Chris before. Nor had he seemed to notice her. But by the time the car stopped at Edith's house that night, Chris was madly in love with Edith, so he said. Edith was aquiver with a new excitement that she thought must be the real thing at last. Was this love? Or was it not the kind of attraction of male to female that was released by touch and pressure as she sat upon his lap? Whether or not this fascination which started with physical stimulation ever could become real love in a fuller sense would depend a great deal upon Edith and Chris. But in itself, sex attraction alone is not love.[1]

Almost everyone experiences these kind of transitory romances, yet if marriage takes place where only infatuation exists, marital disaster lies ahead.

Because we don't know what love is, it can be confused with other emotions. Idealistic romance, feelings of physical attraction, sexual arousal — all these have been mistaken for love.

In the last chapter, my friend Tom talked of falling in love at first sight; this frequent malady is most often cured at the sight of another attractive woman.

While love at first sight worked for Tom and his wife, whose love has grown stronger and more resilient over the years, for too many others "falling in love" begins and ends with the notion of helpless irresponsibility.

The dimensions of love

Some people seem determined to live by this fatalistic concept of love. Love is something over which we exercise no control. It grabs us by the heart — or glands — and we are hooked. Love is a trap we fall *into,* and may fall *out of* just as easily when the storm of emotion passes.

This is not true love, tough love. It is superficial infatuation hiding from reality. Like the old saying, this kind of love is "blind in one eye and doesn't see so well out of the other."

Real love doesn't overcome people and leave them helpless victims at the mercy of their emotions. We might expect this to be the television version of love, but it is not the enduring kind. Real love mixes head *and* heart, passion *and* reason. The love that endures includes thoughtful romance, sensible passion, intelligent emotion. It is built upon spiritual character and sexual integrity.

Samson's passion for women had little to do with reason. His story, found in Judges 14 through 16, has been reinterpreted and retold countless times, not only in tribute to Samson's bravery and strength, but in illustration of his romantic folly as well.

Samson's randy behavior began in his youth, when he "fell in love" with the first of his Philistine women. He married the girl over his parent's objections; they urged him to take a wife from among the people of God instead of from among their heathen overlords.

At his wedding feast Samson challenged the Philistines to a wager. If they could figure out the riddle he posed for them before the seven day celebration ended, he would lose the bet. If not, they would lose. The men threatened his bride and her family if she did not find out the answer to the riddle from Samson and tell them.

She pleaded with Samson throughout the seven days and wore him down with her tears. On the last day, he told her and she passed it on to the men, who demanded the payment of the wager.

What Samson had planned as a happy celebration turned into high tragedy. In his fierce anger, Samson raided a nearby Philistine village, killing thirty of the residents and looting their possessions to pay his debt. It was the beginning of Samson's war with the enemies of his people. It ended twenty years later with his capture and death through his passion for another Philistine woman, Delilah.

Passion or reason?

Logic and reason don't fit with our modern ideas of love. We want the passion without having to put much thought into it. Love with reason sounds cold, emotionless. Yet love without reason hasn't the strength to tough it through the storms any lasting relationship must endure.

Differences of opinion are normal to a marriage. Our differences add color and dimension to life. It is unreasonable to expect the one you love to agree with everything you say and do, so be prepared in courtship to find and explore your differences as well as the things you agree about.

Marital bliss is based on love, but it is love that acknowledges the rights of the other to be his or her own kind of person. Even in matters of faith it is probable you will differ on some issues. As long as you share whole-hearted commitment to God, your different perspectives can only serve to help you both grow in understanding your faith.

It is not easy to keep conflict on a reasoning level. Our emotions are part of the way we shape reality, so it's no surprise that emotional differences will arise. Lovers can and will differ sharply on a number of things. But always remember to give the other person the respect you want for your own views.

This does not mean you should compromise your own moral and ethical points of view. Not at all. But if your differences are found on the moral and ethical level, *don't you think it's better to find out about these differences before you marry?* That is why I believe it absolutely necessary to investigate each other's views intelligently during courtship.

Love is not just physical attraction, although being attracted to one another doesn't hurt a bit!

Love isn't just sexual intimacy, although sex can certainly put the icing on the cake.

Love is never only an emotional feeling, although if the emotions aren't involved, "love" is cold.

Love is not overlooking differences just for the sake of getting along, although differences should be respected.

Love is not simply a matter of shared interests,

though sharing an interest adds compatibility to companionship.

Love is not just a satisfying friendship, although without such a friendship love has little to grow on.

Love is not dependent on compatibility in religious backgrounds, though a shared religion is vital to a healthy relationship.

God is love, and there is something uniquely holy about his love. Perhaps the most eloquent attempt at an explanation of God's kind of love is to be found in Saint Paul's first letter to the Corinthians:

> If I speak with the eloquence of men and of angels, but have no love, I become no more than blaring brass or crashing cymbal. If I have the gift of foretelling the future and hold in my mind not only all human knowledge but the very secrets of God, and if I also have that absolute faith which can move mountains, but have no love, I amount to nothing at all. If I dispose of all that I possess, yes, even if I give my own body to be burned (as a sacrifice), but have no love, I achieve precisely nothing.
> This love of which I speak is slow to lose patience—it looks for a way of being constructive. It is not possessive; it is neither anxious to impress nor does it cherish inflated ideas of its own importance.
>
> Love has good manners and does not pursue selfish advantage. It is not touchy. It does

> not keep account of evil or gloat over the wickedness of other people. On the contrary, it is glad with all good men when truth prevails.
>
> Love knows no limit to its endurance, no end to its trust, no failing of its hope; it can outlast anything. It is, in fact, the one thing that still stands when all else has fallen (1 Corinthians 13: 1-8, Phillips).

Love is God's gift of his presence, turning passion into compassion, drawing harmony out of contrast, changing loneliness into companionship. Anything less than God's kind of love will not weather the stresses, strains and trials that come to all marriages.

We need to face the reality that we are imperfect; we all make mistakes, none of us is sprouting wings. No one is an angel. You might not discover any imperfection in your sweetheart before marriage, but you certainly will find some after the honeymoon — just when your own faults are beginning to stand out in all their glory. That is when real love is needed for survival in marriage.

• Real love overlooks minor irritations. Some men are slobs when they get married and need to be housebroken. It's irritating to have to clean up the hair left in the shower, or put the cap back on the toothpaste. Love has patience, and the ability to demand cooperation.

• Love enables you to forgive, and go on from there. Without letting down personal standards, love enjoys being merciful and challenging. The other person may need forgiveness many times; love makes it possible to forgive as often as necessary and then some.

• Love helps couples face reality. Life is tough enough without adding the burden of romantic illusions. So love knows when to sacrifice personal dreams for immediate necessities, and how to make the sacrifices without looking like a martyr and demanding that the other person feel guilty.

• Love unites and deepens the bond which otherwise might break under stress and strain. A crying baby, sickness, or financial problems can be hard on a relationship if true love is not present to hold you together. But life always has its struggles, and facing them with the resilience of love will strengthen how you feel about each other.

In concluding this chapter, let 's see if there are some ways you might be able to tell if you are truly in love—and if your beloved is truly in love with you. As Evelyn Millis Duvall points out:

> ...there is no quick and easy trick for testing love that will work reliably. Young people will continue to pull daisy petals and cross out letters in each other's names, seek fortune tellers, read tea leaves, and play all the other games that are such fun. But when it comes down to seriously deciding whether we are really in love or not, we turn to more reliable evidences....
>
> Lasting love is too precious to confuse with any of its dazzling substitutes.[2]

If real, true love exists, then the following statements are true about your relationship—*for both of you*.

1. You are happier in the presence of your beloved than when you are with anyone else.

2. There is a feeling of unrest and dissatisfaction when you are apart for any length of time. Your beloved is on your subconscious mind. You write each other often or talk on the telephone.

3. You are physically attracted to each other. Even though neither one of you is a perfect physical specimen, you like each other's looks.

4. You are comfortable in the other's presence. You find lot's of things to do and say together. Even silence is something you can enjoy together.

5. There is an eagerness to share each other's experiences. You are interested in each other's careers, hobbies, opinions, fears, dreams, goals. You can't wait to tell each other what's going on in your lives.

6. You are proud of each other's character and achievements. He is her hero; she is his heroine. There is an eagerness to talk up the fine points of your beloved.

7. There is an unselfishness toward your sweetheart. You will gladly sacrifice your time, your interests, your very self for your beloved. Love does not center on self but on the one loved.

8. You share an eager desire for the success and happiness of the beloved. Each of you works to enhance every opportunity the other has to achieve his or her dreams and goals.

9. You each respect the opinion and judgment of the other and seek each other's advice. You enjoy each other's confidence.

10. You enjoy genuine companionship at all times; you like doing things together, even just being together.

11. You feel a need to pray together, worship together, experience your spiritual pilgrimage together. You are enriched by the other's faith-life, and you are free to share your own.

True love will change your perspectives, no doubt about it. Genuine love creates a "we" feeling. You are no longer I-centered when you're in love. All your planning now is for two instead of one.

Take your courting seriously and go into it with an intelligent, spiritual mind. You are working toward something with eternal implications. What you do in your dating and courting now will affect the life of you and your future spouse—and your descendants. Your church, your community and your world will be forever influenced by how you approach the sanctity of marriage.

1. Evelyn Millis Duvall, *Facts of Life and Love* (New York: Associated Press, International Committee of Young Men's Chriatian Association, 1950) p. 220.

2. Ibid, p. 235

Now that you're engaged

10

Engagement is a definite mutual agreement, an understanding by a couple that they intend to marry. You have decided you enjoy each other's company; you are truly in love and have enough in common to build a happy life together as husband and wife.

The reason you become engaged is to declare to your friends and families that each of you feels you have found the person you should marry. Furthermore, the engagement period gives you time to make the mutual adjustments necessary in beginning a life together, to affirm and agree on the matter of children, your lifestyle, your career dreams and your faith.

In the course of events, you'll set the date and make plans for the wedding, your honeymoon and the start of your life together.

You should look at engagement as the second phase of your maturing commitment to each other. First you met and dated frequently. Along the way, your relationship deepened through mutual attraction and interest to the beginnings of love.

Now you are ready to pledge your lives to each other, to engage each other for life. You will fulfill the pledge you now make to each other in the exchange of vows on your wedding day.

Bonding process

Some have suggested that engagement is the time to try out how you get along sexually. Sexual intercourse is part of the bonding process in marriage. Testing your sexual relationship beforehand will diminish your ability to live up to the tough commitments you'll face when you *are* married. Bonding in commitment is vital to a successful marriage.

I don't think it's just coincidence that the number of divorces has increased at the same time as sexual activity before marriage has increased.

Waiting for sex until marriage isn't going to be easy in our sex-saturated culture, but it's worth it. For health reasons alone, it's worth it. But when you add the invaluable reality that bonding is deepened and enhanced by waiting, then sex before marriage can be seen for the tragic error it has become.

Today a lot of people begin marriage with the idea in mind, "if this doesn't work out, I can always bail out." Bonding isn't 'til death do us part, but for as long as convenient. Persons with a number of previous sexual partners have already gone through the bond breaking process several times.

Now if the Bible account is true—and millions of married couples over the centuries have proven it to be so—then we are meant to leave father and mother and become one flesh with only one spouse.

I am aware that some marriages become a no-man's-land of conflict. I am aware some are based on fraudulent misrepresentation of one or even both of the parties involved. I am aware that the oldest traditions of the Christian church allow such marriages to be dissolved or annuled.

But that is not the original concept. Some Pharisees came to Jesus one day to try and upset his influence with the people. They asked him if it was lawful for a man to divorce his wife.

> "What did Moses command you?" he replied.
>
> They said, "Moses permitted a man to write a certificate of divorce and send her away."
>
> "It was because your hearts were hard that Moses wrote you this law," Jesus replied. "But at the beginning of creation God 'made them male and female.' 'For this reason a man will leave his father and mother and be united to his wife, and the two will become one flesh.' So they are no longer two but one. Therefore what God has joined together, let man not separate."
>
> When they were in the house again, the disciples asked Jesus about this. He answered, "Anyone who divorces his wife and marries another woman commits adultery against her. And if she divorces her husband and marries another man, she commits adultery" (Mark 10: 2-12, NIV).

Sexual integrity is vital to a successful marriage, starting long before the wedding. Because of its function in bonding, sex must be reserved for marriage. Therefore the engagement period is essential for you as a time to be sure your relationship has what it takes to survive, *before* the bonding takes place.

Marriage is much more than fun and games in bed. If you stop to think about it, the husband-wife union is the fundamental building block of civilization. There are no associations of accountability smaller in size than the married couple. And society is moral or immoral depending on whether marriage is held to moral or immoral standards.

But beyond the moral and ethical values of society, there are practical considerations too. Let's look at a few:–

1. Children who are deprived of the bonds of holy matrimony are psychologically wounded, and have a much more difficult time in achieving maturity than those who grow up in the care of a loving well-bonded couple.

The engagement period is time to find out each other's expectations about children. We hear a lot about family planning and the population explosion and how expensive it is to bring a child into the world today.

Yet it has never been "economical" to have a child, there has always been a physical and emotional cost, as well as the monetary one. So don't be overly impressed by such propaganda. Having children is still one of the two most important reasons to get married, the other being companionship.

2. So prepare yourselves now to accept the responsibilities of childbirth, it's a perfectly natural result of married love. Don't count on even the most recent birth control techniques, none are 100 percent effective. And if you anticipate abortion as the ultimate in birth control, think again. For a Christian,

life is precious, and you may put yourself in an untenable situation if your spouse demands abortion and you cannot face the guilt. Get this out in the open before getting into a marriage you may regret.

3. How do you feel about husband-wife roles? Our civilization is somewhere in a reshuffle of possibilities for women's work outside the home and men's work inside the home. With the development of technologies to make homecare duties less time consuming, the husband can wash clothes and turn on the microwave as easily as the wife.

One of the unexpected results of the women's revolution is that it has not brought the freedom wives were expecting. Not only are they working outside the home, women are continuing to do most of the work inside the home too.

You may have perspectives on this the other doesn't share. Talk them through. As you explore your differences—and the things on which you agree—you will grow to understand each other and learn from each other.

4. Now is the time to come to an understanding on what each of you expects to accomplish in life. Careers can go in opposite directions and tear you apart, if you haven't established an understanding of priorities for each of you. I've seen enough in my counseling to believe a couple can hold widely divergent career goals and still enjoy deep satisfaction in their marriage. But the basis for happiness in such a union comes from a foundation of trust, loyalty, honesty and respect.

For a great many women homemaking and child rearing demand the full exercise of a wide range of abilities and talents. It is an unfortunate consequence of our modern technological civilization that women who delight in this demanding career are made to feel inferior. Somehow women who have a career are esteemed higher than those who give their lives to produce character and integrity in their children.

Yet it's an advantage for any woman to be trained in a marketable skill. Before her marriage Ann had worked in real estate. After years of happy family life, her husband contracted Alzheimer's disease. She cared for him at home as long as possible, until his mindless strength became more than she could handle. Then she placed him in a nursing home, and returned to the real estate business.

Now she is able to visit him daily, and her earnings are gradually reducing the load of debt that piled up during his long illness.

5. Financial problems destroy as many marriages as sexual infidelity. How much will you need to earn to live where you plan to live? Is your budget feasible? Can you even put together a budget?

It is NOT true that two can live as cheaply as one. You are venturing into unknown territory, where you have not been before. You don't know each other's spending habits, and little about each other's expectations. You need to find out as much as you can about budgets from a lot of sources, parents, friends, your banker. Dig out some reference books at the library. Don't spend all of your time on romance, you may not be able to afford it later.

I don't want you to put a price on your relationship. Yet you do need to know where you are heading; if the one you love is financially irresponsible, now is the time to find out, not when you are facing bankruptcy later and hating him or her for it.

6. A major item to talk about now is where you plan to live. Close to folks? At college? Are you prepared to make career moves?

One couple I know have moved nineteen times, twelve times after they had begun to have children. The experience encouraged a feeling of rootlessness. The question,"how long are we going to be here?" inhibited their ability to relate to any one community. Yet they enjoyed the variety and living in a number of locales has given them a broader outlook than most of their contemporaries.

If you want to see the world and your betrothed longs to stay put, you have some negotiations to work through. If you are to be happy, both of you should agree on how you intend to reconcile your differences. Don't count on one of you doing all the giving and the other all the taking.

7. Your engagement should give you the opportunity to evaluate each other's dreams and goals. It's a time-worn word, but "lifestyle" describes it appropriately. In romance novels a princess can marry a plowboy and live happily ever after, but in real life, wide differences in lifestyles—or lifestyle goals—can be virtually impossible barriers to a happy life together. It's possible to trust the spirit of God or to follow the spirit of our materialistic world, but not both at the same time (see Matthew 6:24).

8. Above all else, your engagement will give you the time to confirm that God has led you together and is continuing to lead you in your plans. This is

tricky, because all of your emotions are apt to be riding high and it's easy to misinterpret good feelings as God's blessing. But you should allow enough time to be sure; that is what an engagement is for.

Nearly all studies of happy marriages show that the factors which make for success are already at work *before* the wedding day. In a similar way the factors which create unsuccessful marriages exist in the relationship during dating and engagement. So now is the time to look closely at your relationship. An engagement is a serious commitment, but it is not as permanent as the bonds of matrimony.

At this point, if you think you can change the other person's way of thinking and behaving, think again. Even God has a hard time making people over into what they really are—and if he is having trouble with your friend, you don't stand a chance.

Similarly, you may believe the other person is as you *hope* he or she is. We like to project onto other people what we expect them to be, and refuse to accept what they really are. So now is the time to take off the "rose colored glasses" and see the other person clearly, honestly. You might even like that person better than the one you imagine. At least you won't be fooling yourself, and demanding the other person live up to your unreal expectations.

It takes a certain amount of maturity (translate: common sense experience) to be able to step back from your deep emotional involvement and thoughtfully assess your relationship.

The world out there is a tough place for the tender shoots of a new marriage. Even persons who have been out of school for a number of years find it difficult; young people still in school have too limited an exposure to the world to be able to judge how their relationships will survive in it. So it's no surprise that teen-age marriages have a high rate of failure; what is surprising is that some succeed.

How long should your engagement last? Long enough to do the work we have been talking about in this chapter. But not so long that physical desire can betray you into sexual intimacies before the day set for your wedding.

Let's sum up what you should expect for your engagement:–

1. Sorry, no sex. Not yet. Hang on to your sexual integrity until you can bond your relationship after you exchange your wedding vows.

2. Confirm your choice of the person you'll spend the rest of your life with, by thoughtful examination of who this beloved person really is. Find out the essentials *now*.

3. Understand each other's points of view on career goals, children, lifestyle, and above all else, faith. *Don't* let your emotions rule your head on these matters; you'll live to regret it.

4. In fact, you'll need to agree that you are heading in the same direction together, that you have similar convictions on spiritual matters, lifestyle, ethical and moral concerns. Remember, "A house divided against itself cannot stand."

5. Decide now that the person you've begun to see clearly is worth the rest of your life. Accept the fact you will not be able to change the other into your image of what he or she should be. Don't play God

in the other's life, God can do it so much better.

6. Make sure there are no residual lovers hanging around to muddy the tranquil sea of matrimony. If either of you have an old flame, be sure to put out the fire now.

7. Take charge of your own wedding plans. Be sure it's all that you hoped it would be in the way of a celebration, but *don't* put yourselves or your parents in debt. Some of the most beautiful weddings in which I have officiated have been sublimely simple and economical.

8. Get to know your future in-laws, they will be part of your family from now on.

9. Review and reshape the vows you will take to each other and make them your own.

10. Learn to share decisions. It's time to establish the "we" feeling together. Love, respect and appreciation for each other will deepen as your sense of companionship grows.

As you near the day of your wedding, you will experience second thoughts. Examine them to be sure they are not just cold feet. Everybody has second thoughts, and as long as your concerns don't come from questions about the character and spiritual substance of your betrothed, you will survive. Strong, maturing love overcomes fear and takes the steps of faith as God leads to a lasting, happy marriage.

Holy Matrimony

11

The day arrives. You have done your homework. In the weeks and months of your engagement your love has grown stronger, your respect for each other has deepened, and your trust in each other has been confirmed.

You are ready now to move on into the holy experience of marriage, made whole by your sexual integrity and spiritual fidelity, blessed of God in your intentions together and your obedience to his Spirit.

If you have planned well for the occasion, you remain in control of the wedding celebration. Let your friends know clearly what you expect from them. Some weddings have been spoiled by the exuberant shenanigans of friends who paint the bridegroom's car, tear up luggage, and create havoc all in the name of fun. Don't let it happen.

Set the spiritual tone of the celebration ahead of time. Don't let it degenerate into a contest of who can cause the most embarrassment. How? Let me make a few suggestions, in the way of the accounts of three different weddings. In each, control was maintained by the couple from beginning to end.

Anna and Paul planned the kind of wedding most of their college friends would be accustomed to, with matron of honor, bridesmaids, best man, groomsmen, flower girl, ring bearer, formal attire, and a reception after in the church hall. But they kept it simple.

Instead of the expense of special gowns, they asked their attendants to join them in simplicity and wear "something old, something new, something special, something blue." Anna and Paul found out what each had chosen to wear in each category and listed these as a part of the wedding invitations sent to their many friends.

Some of their friends had little money to spare, so in their invitations Anna urged everyone to come without feeling the demand to bring a present. Yet knowing that most would make an effort to get them something, she included suggestions for gifts under $10.

In the invitations Paul told friends of their plans to be driven to the bus station by his new father-in-law, and asked them to refrain from doing anything to the car or following them to the station; they were concerned for everyone's safety in traffic. Instead, it would be his joy and Anna's if they would join with them in making this day a holy memory.

The wedding became a holy memory for a lot of their friends because of their simple, direct and honest approach.

Joyce and Alec teach music and they chose to be married in a park one Saturday afternoon in May. A group of friends provided the music, and the couple sang their vows to each other. Their minister surprised them by performing part of the ceremony in the form of a medieval chant—he had practiced for several weeks.

Joyce's family provided a buffet of salads and fruits; Alec's family invited several music groups and the reception became a joyous musical picnic in the open air.

Naomi and Scott are deeply committed members of a small community church. They chose to exchange their vows during the Sunday morning worship service, as an expression of life shared in the fellowship of believers. The congregational liturgy that morning included a series of Biblical references on marriage, and married couples were invited to renew their vows.

The congregation was also invited to break bread with the newly married couple afterward, during a meal of fish, rice, vegetables, and homemade breads.

What these examples show is that there is no one way to plan for your wedding. In fact there are as many different possibilities for your wedding as your creativity can come up with. Yet there are factors common to each of the three examples I would like you to notice.

1. Each wedding plan came out of what the couple were like in themselves. None followed a program outlined for them by wedding counselors or bridal magazines.

2. Attendants were not asked to buy or rent expensive clothes for only one occasion. One couple even asked friends to come without gifts; often a wedding invitation is seen as an unspoken demand

for an expensive wedding present.

3. Each ceremony focused on spiritual values of friendship, sharing, and love.

4. In every case, the couple maintained control of their wedding, including the expense.

5. Each wedding became the joyous, memorable occasion the couple desired. You can make yours as wholesome.

6. This point is not as obvious, but if you were to ask each couple, they would affirm that God had led them together, and would continue to be their Lord and guide in the future as he had been in their plans to marry. How they explain their relationship to God is different, but the message is the same—God is with them, present in their lives.

In your marriage, what each of you brings to the union will be unique. I know it's not popular with some to talk about the differences between male and female, because it may raise some of the old prejudices. Nevertheless, there *are* differences, wonderful differences. Male and female biology alone can create a host of contrasts. Add genetic traits, hormonal levels and inherited singularities, and the possibility for difference is limitless.

You will have years together to discover what it really means to be male and female. Maleness and femaleness is not so much genital, although our reproductive equipment is certainly a part. The traits for mothering are not exclusively female, and there are countless women who have shown remarkable abilities for family leadership, usually perceived as a male prerogative.

My counsel is not to worry too much about male-female roles, and whether you fit the image of your friends and relatives. Be yourselves. Share with each other the hundreds of tasks that go into home-making and building a family. A husband can cook and clean and feed babies, a wife can repair plumbing, do carpentry and wash the car. You don't *have* to share in order to be happy together, but doing so helps build understanding.

Somewhere deep in the shadows of human history, it became a cultural "law" that men hunted and women did "women's work"—grinding grain, cooking, tending the children. It was a good working relationship, based on the difference in size and strength between husband and wife.

Much physical work today still can be categorized by size and strength, so some men are more suited to some jobs than some women. But those distinctions are not as important as they were in the past

New level of relationship

The Bible often reflects the roles of men and women as they were in the distant past. In the earliest times, a man who could afford them could have several wives. As cultures developed, women were sheltered from public exposure. Women did not take part in public debate; clothing veiled them from head to toe.

In the New Testament church, women were lifted to a new level, as full participants in Christ. "All of you who were baptized 'into' Christ have put on the family likeness of Christ. Gone is the distinction between Jew and Greek, slave and free man, male and female—you are all one in Christ Jesus" (Galatians 3:27, 28, Phillips translation).

Now the divine privilege of love sets wife and husband free of cultural "law." Now you are free to submit yourselves, each to the other, out of reverence for the presence of God in your marriage. It won't be easy to do, because we are accustomed to looking after our own personal demands.

In marriage the two have become one; the *union* is now to be your central concern. The other person's integrity is now coalesced with yours. The husband, far from going his own way and doing his own thing, is now called upon to love his wife "as Christ loved the church and gave himself up for her" (Galatians 5:25). The wife, far from resenting anyone interfering with her life, is now to submit to her husband, "as to the Lord" (Galatians 5:22).

Being subject to each other isn't a matter of abdicating responsibility for your own integrity. On the contrary, you are called, nay, *challenged* by the living God to put all your energies to work to make the new union an evidence of his grace and love. Together—with God—you can become more than the sum of two parts.

Submit to each other in all things, not just a few. Be guided by each other *as by the Lord* in the work you do, in how you live, in the friends you make, the hobbies you follow, the way you spend your money as well as the way you make it.

God can speak more clearly through the two of you as to what he expects of the "one" of you than he can to each of you individually. Listen to him, with care and in obedience. Make it a demand upon your time—upon your life- together.

Submit to each other sexually. Now is the pay off for waiting; you can look upon the magnificent emotions of sexual intimacy as God's gift to you both for your sexual integrity. Now the integrity of each can link with the other in the bonds of *holy* matrimony.

Enjoy each other. Rejoice in each other. The powerful joys of sex are yours, bringing strength in your love, peace in your relationship, hope in your abilities together to do all that God has for you to do.

If you submit yourselves and your marriage to God, he is wonderfully able to keep you and bless you in every good thing as a demonstration of his grace. In Christ you have his forgiveness, in the Spirit you have his power to lift you above every weakness and sin.

Let me close with the great prayer of the apostle Paul, as my prayer for you and your marriage:–

> For this reason I kneel before the Father, from whom his whole family in heaven and on earth derives its name. I pray that out of his glorious riches he may strengthen you with power through his Spirit in your inner being, so that Christ may dwell in your hearts through faith. And I pray that you, being rooted and established in love, may have the power, together with all the saints, to grasp how wide and long and high and deep is the love of Christ, and to know this love that surpasses knowledge—that you may be filled to the measure of all the fulness of God.
>
> Now to him who is able to do immeasurably more than all we ask or imagine, according to

his power that is at work within us, to him be glory in the church and in Christ Jesus throughout all generations, forever and ever! Amen (Ephesians 3:14-21, NIV).